The Overcomer's Life

The Reality of Redemption

ALEXANDER O. EMOGHENE

THE OVERCOMERS LIFE

The Reality of Redemption
Alexander O. Emoghene

Tulip Publications
Ceintuurbaan 23b
3051AG
Rotterdam

Web: Tulippublications.com
Claypotchurchint.com
ISBN: 978-90-824117-7-5
Cover Design & Page Layout By: www.madeforministry.co.uk

Table of Contents

THE OVERCOMERS LIFE

1 John 5:4: For whatever is born of God overcomes the world: and this is the victory that overcomes the world, even our faith.

John 3:16: except a man is born-again he cannot see the kingdom of God.

The new birth is not just a change of mind or a change of opinion. Many may have imagined that it is switching lifestyles, moving out of profane circles and into sacred ones. Some use terms like, 'try Jesus and see what will happen in your life' as though Christ is a momentary pill that may or may not work or a jacket that can be tossed on and off at whim. The trouble here is that the emphasis is on the temporal; a person is not encouraged to look at the new birth in light of eternity but rather the 'here-and-now'. An individual with such a mind-set, will soon find out that their relationship with the Father will be inconsistent and go from hot to cold in a short space of time.

The new birth is a change in nature, a transformation and to fully understand it we must first understand the term 'born-again.' So, what is being born-again? Let's start by defining the word 'born'. Dictionary.com defines born as brought forth from birth. This means an individual who was not visible or in existence was brought forth into existence by birth.

Biologically, we all understand the process of a woman conceiving. At her due time, labour kicks in and she gives birth to her baby. This baby has never been in the world before and at the moment of birth he or she steps into and is given sight of a new world and a new life.

Let's see this process from the baby's perspective. Here is a new life, totally new to this world. A life that has never seen this side of the world before but now she or he is brought forth in it; taken from one world or location and positioned in a different one. Up until now birth, the baby's reality was limited to a small space the baby called home. Their mother's womb was the only world they knew. Unknown to the baby, there is a much larger world to discover. Though it may be invisible and unrealistic to the baby, it is as real as their present reality.

Therefore, the born-again experience can be understood by this biological reality. When an individual is born anew they are literally born into a new world of the spirit. Which, up until the moment one gives their life to the lordship of Jesus Christ, was not real. Once a person is born-again, the new world is made real, reachable and revolutionary.

Another truth is that at birth, a healthy baby is born complete with all they need. They have all their vital organs, tissue, cells etc. – everything they need to function in this world. This is a crucial revelation because at the point of birth no organ will be added to a healthy baby. Yes, we know that the body will grow and develop but for the sake of illustration, at birth the process is completed. In the same vein, the born-again child of God is completely born into the image of God.

Let's take a closer look at the other word 'again'. From dictionary.com, we see synonyms of the word such as; to be new, another time and once more. We can define the word 'again' as to repeat something. If we put these two words together we are confronted with this spiritual reality which is to be brought forth from birth another time.

This concept of a new birth caused Nicodemus to ask Jesus 'how can a man be born-again while he is old' (John 3:4). Certainly, Nicodemus was somewhat spiritually literate and so his question was logical, just and came from a desire to truly understand. Jesus had to expound to this learned teacher the true revelation of being born-again. Jesus went on to explain that it was possible spiritually, this is because people get born-again by faith through the power of the Holy Spirit. Jesus described this new birth as being born-again. It is a term that visually depicts one being born-again from God through the womb of faith by the power of the Holy Spirit.

There is a link between the new birth and mind renewal. The changing of the mind, or renewing the mind, is a process that every believer must undergo, and the process of mind renewal is a life-long journey. When a person is born-again it is not just about a change of mind, that is why some say, 'I have tried Church, but now I desire something else'. Friends, no matter how hard a baby imagines being in the womb they cannot go back there. Being born-again is similar in the sense that it is not just religion or philosophy.

If you truly become born-again a transformation takes place, whether it is visible to the natural eye or not because you have stepped into a new life in God.

The believer is born of God. They are born into a new spiritual world, the world of God, and can participate in the life of God. They are born into a newness of life with a full and perfect spirit; one that reflects the love and grace of God and is ready to grow in the things of God. If this is not your reality, then it is possible that regeneration has not taken place. You may have stepped into religion, but not regeneration; there has not been a new birth.

As a born-again believer, you can begin enjoying your new life with God even while on planet earth – you do not have to wait until you get to heaven! The born-again life is not just a culture shift, it is being born into a new divine culture, one that has never been experienced by the individual. It is new; it is a totally new space waiting for the believer to develop his or her faith. Every believer must make a conscience decision to walk in all the greatness that they have come into as a result faith in God; the walk is one of victory, peace and joy.

The new believer has been emptied from this worlds influence and desires, and they have been endued with heavens influence and desires. They have stepped from darkness into light, sin has lost it control and they now operate from the place of right standing with God. Just like the baby was emptied from the womb; the world, your previous womb, has lost you. You are no more of the world, even though you are in this world bodily, your spirit is nowhere to be found in worldly realms anymore. (John 17:16: John 15:19).

Jesus said that he who is born of the flesh is flesh (meaning by a woman through the womb) and he who born of the Spirit is spirit (meaning born through God by the womb of faith). All humans must participate in the human experience because we must all first be born naturally. These experiences vary from person to person and can be drastically different. Nevertheless, they are all real human experiences.

I'm sure you have heard it said before, but it warrants repeating; you do not choose how you come into this world, but you choose where and how you will spend eternity. Your eternity is determined by the choices you make in the here and now. Never ever forget that!

THE GREAT ESCAPE

The scripture declares the whole world is under wickedness (1 John 5:19). The wicked one here is a reference to the devil (satan). All those in this world or bound to this worldly system are under his power, control, dominion, and rulership.

The enemy's power is heavy in the world and he holds people all around the world in spiritual prisons. From physical prisons of sickness and disease, to emotional prisons of depression and stress. He rules with fear and paralyses people with demonic control. But there is hope – there is a way out!

A born-again person has escaped from the wicked one and has been born into the kingdom of His dear Son (Colossians 1:13). As you walk in the new life, it is in this place that the Bible says, God keeps you safe (1 John 5:18).

1 Peter 1:4 says, 'Whereby are given unto us exceeding great and precious promises: that by these ye might be partakes of His divine nature, having escaped the corruption that is in the world through lust.'

The believer has escaped from the major weapons of satan which he uses to oppress every inhabitant in the world who is not born-again. (Hebrews 2:15). Dictionary.com defines fear as an unpleasant emotion caused by the threat of danger, pain or harm. From this definition we can truly appreciate the fact that the whole world, those that are not born-again, suffer acutely at the hands of satan; Why? Because by nature, the greatest of fear is the fear of death (1 Corinthians 15:26).

It is from the fear of death that other forms of fear are derived; the fear of sickness, fear of the unknown, fear of the unexpected, fear of rejection, fear of failure, fear of pain, and so forth. Fear is founded on death and ultimately causes it.

Fear is a spiritual prison or spiritual pit, where satan holds his victims under severe pressure. This pressure may manifest itself as the desires of living a pretentious life in hypocrisy, lies and temptation. Sooner or later these individuals will find themselves helplessly trapped in unrighteousness and ungodly ways – promoting the works of evil.

Thank God that through the new birth, Christ has become the believer's life (Colossians 3:4) and death and the fear of death has lost its grip on the heart and the mind of the believer forever. God has now brought comfort and assurance where doubt and uncertainty once was. Where the fear of damnation dwelt, eternal life has now been born and it has swallowed up death for good (John 3:16). We have escaped from satan's prison, or pit as it were, to the glorious liberty of His dear Son (Galatians 5:1). Because of the new birth, we step out of prison and step into freedom!

ESCAPE FROM CORRUPTION

The scripture is so clear about the corruption that is in the world. The word 'corruption' means to perish or destroy. It also means to batter or spoil. These are all synonyms to satan's name 'abaddon' (Revelation 9:1).The enemy's hidden agenda is to take good things and abuse them until they lose all value. He steals, spoils, corrupts and destroys (John 10:10).

We have brilliant individuals that have not entered the new birth and are led by satan to several paths that will only ever lead to destruction and eternal damnation. Talents are wasted because of destructive habits, and they become a menace to their relatives and society at large. It was never meant to be this way, God has created each of us with a great plan – but we must choose to walk in it to see the reality of His master plan manifest in our lives.

Lifestyles such as pornography, smoking, drinking, gambling, stealing, lying and cheating are used by satan to trap his victims. This becomes a continuous cycle of addiction which leads to heavy guilt, shame and regret. The enemy desires to stop personal development and growth, his plan is that you regress and get worse not progress and get better. (Luke 16:13)

The good news is that the believer has escaped, and received divine immunity from these corruptions; satan has no influence any longer except that which is given to him. You must shut down and resist him at every given opportunity and he will flee from you.

I would really like to encourage you here that no matter where you are in this life, Jesus is here for you and by faith you can receive His grace to be made new; you can be born-again! (Romans 10:13).

ESCAPE FROM HELL

Another reality is the escape from eternal misery in hell. For the born-again believer, the escape from this corruption is real, refreshing and provokes joy and gladness of heart. In addition, it is this escape from eternal damnation and the promise for life everlasting in Christ, that stimulates the thirst to follow after Christ. This thirst equips the believer to hold on to a strong hope and confidence in living the righteous life here on earth.

This assurance is captured John 1:12: 'But as many as receive him, to them gave he power to become the sons of God, even to them that believe.' Your faith in Christ has brought in the house as it were. The born-again believer is no longer a slave or a servant but a Son or daughter of God. The believer is now granted, by grace, to be born into the family of God.

There are divine experiences that one can only experience due to this new life. It is a new place. It grows and blossoms by spiritual default as it were, it is not by effort anymore but it is by spiritual nature. The nature of God indwells the believer and it is time to grow in the grace of God (2 Peter 3:18).

Psalm 66:8: You made men ride over our heads; we went through fire and through water, yet you brought us out into a place of abundance.

It is very important I mention here that you have not simply escaped the wicked one (satan), the fear of death, corruption and eternal damnation which is in this world; you have also been positioned to enjoy the great privileges of the Kingdom of God.

2 Corinthians 13:14: The grace of the Lord Jesus Christ, and the love of God, and the communion of the Holy Ghost, be with you all. Amen.

This is what I call the place of abundance, a place where – being a child of God, you have access to:

1. The grace of the Lord Jesus
2. The love of God
3. The fellowship of the Holy Spirit

THE GRACE OF THE LORD JESUS CHRIST

The new birth ushers the believer into the world of the grace of the Lord Jesus. This grace of the Lord Jesus Christ reveals the mystery behind the power that enabled the works of Jesus Christ. It points to the mighty power that propelled the incarnation, which meant that for His assignment of redemption, this grace was given to facilitate the awesome process of God becoming flesh:

1 Timothy 3:16: …And without controversy great is the mystery of godliness: God was manifest in the flesh, justified in the Spirit, seen of angels, preached unto the Gentiles, believed on in the world, received up into glory.

In the flesh, grace continued relentlessly in His earthly life and ministry. He led a sinless life (Hebrews 4:15). His messages and His works of miracles were all filled with grace (John 1:14). This grace was active at His trial. In a normal situation, most humans would have died - considering the beatings, torture and loss of blood He endured, but grace was working tirelessly. Oh, even in the death, burial and resurrection of the Lord Jesus Christ grace was available.

1 Corinthians 15:54: So when this corruptible shall have put on incorruption, and this mortal shall have put on immortality, then shall be brought to pass the saying that is written, death is swallowed up in victory.

After His death and burial, it is the same grace that works in the transformation of the body of Jesus Christ that is now clothed with immortality; grace swallowed up death. Well! You may say, 'Alexander, the Holy Spirit did that!' Well the scripture addresses the Holy Spirit as 'the Spirit of Grace' (Hebrews 10:29).

Paul draws the attention of the believer, to this mystery of grace, and how we access it to enjoy the supernatural endowment. The believer has not just come into His life but has also been empowered through His life, just as Jesus was empowered to live a victorious and an overcoming life here on earth.

The grace of the Lord Jesus Christ made all that Jesus Christ did successful. If you look at all that Jesus Christ accomplished here to earth for us, His complete work, the scriptures say it was because of the grace upon His life.

2 Corinthians 8:9: For ye know the grace of our Lord Jesus Christ, that, though he was rich, yet for your sakes, he became poor, that ye through his poverty might be rich.

This is the reality the believer must hunger to conceive; the knowledge of the grace of the Lord Jesus Christ. Paul said, 'for ye know the grace.' Grace means to be divinely enabled or empowered through God's unmerited and unearned favour. God did not just call you for nothing (John 16:15). He has a plan for you, an awesome assignment, a powerful mission and grace has come into your life to help fulfil that assignment.

Grace is working as your read this book. It is His grace that has led you to open this book. You see, His grace will lead you to uncover secrets, to discover the places and people that are instrumental to accomplishing His plan for your life. It means God knows where you are and all you need to be empowered with for your assignment; grace is the carriage that will get you there.

Grace is a gift that comes freely and does all the work for free whilst making you look good. Grace did not fail Jesus Christ and grace will not fail you. Grace makes all knowledge available, it makes all creativity manifest, it makes all understanding flow and all resources reachable. Grace is God's favour and God's blessing on you. This is the grace that has been made available to you as a believer, tell me what can stop you?

Hear what the Apostle Paul said:

1 Corinthians 15:9-11: For I am the least [worthy] of the apostles, who am not fit or deserving to be called an apostle, because I once wronged and pursued and molested the church of God [oppressing it with cruelty and violence]. But by the grace (the unmerited favour and blessing) of God I am what I am, and His grace toward me was not [found to be] for nothing (fruitless and without effect). In fact, I worked harder than all of them [the apostles], though it was not really I, but the grace (the unmerited favour and blessing) of God which was with me. (AMPC)

Yes! You will still need to work on a few things but ultimately you must have this understanding; in the Kingdom of God, He has worked out every detail and it is left for you to understand the concept of receiving, by faith, the grace of the Lord Jesus Christ.

What then is your attitude toward this grace? Your attitude should be a positive one and your response should always be to receive! Listen, with God, you must develop the attitude of receiving because even at your very best, you cannot compete with the grace of God – nothing can.

2 Corinthians 6:1: We then, as workers together with him, beseech you also that ye receive not the grace of God in vain.

When does one receive things in vain? When one fails to use what has been given to them in the appropriate manner or when one is totally ignorant of the value of what has been given. It is possible, through ignorance and a lack of revelation, to live as one who has no grace and go through life as a believer, full of accessible grace but defeated in all areas. I pray this will not be your portion in Jesus Name!

Some, not knowing the value of what they have received, work hard, think hard and end up in hard places. I pray that you will tap into the grace that has been made available to you from now on! It is your time for the grace of the Lord Jesus Christ to take over all your affairs in Jesus Name. Paul urges here that the receiver of grace must walk in grace to the maximum. He did, and his impact is still felt to this day. My prayer is that the grace of the Lord Jesus Christ will have free range in your life, to get the results that God desires for you in Jesus Name. I pray that the grace of the Lord will replace your years of labour with favour.

- Grace will add flavour to your life
- Grace will add colour to your life
- Receive it in Jesus name!

THE LOVE OF GOD

A true encounter with the love of God is where many fall short. Many attempt to approach this side of God in the human realm, with their five senses. Somehow, they conceive that God loves them from a human point of view and in the end try to establish their own righteousness.

Let the love of God have access into to your heart as you read this!

Does the phrase 'the love of God' project how God loves us? Or is it showing Gods love toward us? The scripture declares GOD IS LOVE (1 John 4:8). In other words, the phrase is advancing who God is and not essentially what He does. The phrase 'the love of God' is telling the believer to enter into the world of who God is: HE IS LOVE.

If you can conclude that He is love then nothing will hinder you to understand His motives, His character and His plans for your life. At times, life can get so hard and unbearable and many begin to ask the question why God this and why God that. This line of questioning is always marked with an undertone of 'God does not care about me or love me.'

Friends, God is love! Even on His worst day, if He had one, His love for you would not be affected. He does not just possess love, it is all that He is and that is how He wants to be seen. The new birth makes this encounter possible. Encounter the loving Father today!

Before the new birth, the thought of God excites a feeling of judgment, hypocrisy, anger and many other negative feelings because we were far from Him (Ephesians 2: 11-13). Once you are born-again, the new birth excites a feeling of love, forgiveness, and security. Why? Because of the love of God. The believer is not just loved by God, but the believer now resides in the Father and has taken the same nature of love.

So, from the moment, you experience the new birth God begins to treat you as God would treat His Son. I call it a LOVE EXCLUSIVE. The individual will hear God speak to them as God speaks to Jesus. This is why the scripture calls the believer an overcomer, because of the love of God. The believer gets to hear of higher and greater things that are not from this world. The believer that knows the love of God positions themselves for better and develops a higher esteem in this life. They will constantly hear God speaking good of them and to them. Even where God brings correction, it will be received from the brevity and atmosphere of love.

The love of God allows the believer to walk freely and talk freely with the feeling of forgiveness forever. The love of God generates a powerful spirit of identity and ownership to the things of heaven. 'You belong here,' says God. You have a prepared inheritance. You are His own and He is yours. Like Adam called Eve the bone of his bone and the flesh of his flesh. You are the spirit of His Spirit and this love of God in you, runs deep.

John 17:23: I in them, and thou in me, that they may be made perfect in one; and that the world may know that thou hast sent me, and hast loved them, as thou hast loved me.

Jesus made an outstanding statement here, He concluded that God loves us just as God loves Him! Oh, how we need this perspective in our day. There is no need for performance or trying to buy His love through works anymore. The Bible says 'Which He lavished upon us in every kind of wisdom and understanding (practical insight and prudence)' (Ephesians 1:8 AMPC).

I chose this verse simply for the word 'lavished.' Every time the Lord thinks of us, it is to lavish us with great love, why? He is an abundant God. El Shaddai is His name. What can He not do for you if He loves you as Himself? Think about it; how do you treat yourself when you have a cut or something like that? I am sure you take great care of it and go the necessary lengths to make sure healing will take place.

Often, Jesus' results and demonstrations were because of His awareness of God's love:

John 3:36: The Father loveth the Son, and hath given all things into his hand.

John 15:9: As the Father hath loved me, so have I loved you: continue ye in my love.

John 10:17: For this reason the Father loves Me, because I lay down My life so that I may take it again.

Jesus had a healthy father-and-son mentality and He always functioned under the love of God. All through His ministry here on earth He never departed from the revelation that God is His Father and that God loves Him beyond anything else; this must become the believer's mentality and perspective.

Now read Ephesians 5:9: For no man ever yet hated his own flesh; but nourisheth and cherisheth it, even as the Lord the church:

Love is the motive to nourish and cherish your body that is why you must rest assured that God will nourish and cherish all that concerns you. You are now His body and He is taking care of you – even as you are reading this book. One way He takes care of you is by revealing more of who He is to you.

I pray that His love will flood your heart and mind in Jesus Name.

Matthew 6:31-33: Therefore take no thought, saying, What shall we eat? or, What shall we drink? or, Wherewithal shall we be clothed? For after all these things do the Gentiles seek: for your heavenly Father knoweth that ye have need of all these things. But seek ye first the kingdom of God, and his righteousness, and all these things shall be added unto you.

Jesus reminded the disciples not to worry about anything because it has been taking care of. If God loves Jesus as much as He loves you, then He is always with you, will always provide for you and His presence will terminate the presence of the enemy. I pray that whatever has come to tamper with the love of God in your life is terminated today in Jesus Name!

God's love will surround you from now on, God's love will flow from your inner man unlimited and God's love will break every fear and doubt today in Jesus Name.

God is love – if you are in Him then you are in love!

THE FELLOWSHIP OF THE SPIRIT

Fellowship is where it all begins to happen, it is what makes you unlimited, it is where you learn the voice of God. Get ready for the time of your life; fellowship with God.

What is fellowship? One definition from dictionary.com says it is friendly relationship or companionship. Another definition states it is the associating of persons who have similar interests or taste. What does this mean to you as a new born? It means you have been freely giving access, by the grace of the Lord Jesus Christ in the love of God, to have a friendly relationship with the most powerful Person in the universe, the Holy Spirit.

The believer is called to intimate companionship with the Holy Spirit; unlimited access, to associate with the person of the Holy Spirit. This is God we are talking about. We talk about the grace of the Lord Jesus Christ, the love of God and the person of the Holy Spirit. This means, as believers, we become companions and associates. We are being handed over not just to grace and love but we are now given the freedom to enjoy being in fellowship with the Father, working in partnership with Him on this side of eternity.

Fellowship means you have been raised to become associated with the Holy Spirit. This is an association that will produce the same

results that God needs you to produce –
producing everything God has commanded
from His word.

Do not forget, from the beginning of creation
it was the Holy Spirit who blew over the
earth before creation could be manifested:

Genesis 1:1-2: In the beginning God created
the heaven and the earth. And the earth was
without form, and void; and darkness was
upon the face of the deep. And the Spirit of
God moved upon the face of the waters.

There is a move in your spirit right now and
this move is by association and fellowship. It
begins with your life and then you will be
used as an overflow, to help the lives of
others. I pray your fellowship with the Holy
Spirit will not be in vain.

Through fellowship, there will be an amazing
creative power that will be released into your
heart. Start receiving it NOW! Fellowship
with the Father, the Son and the Holy Spirit

releases power into your spirit because the Holy Spirit is the Spirit of power. This power is the power from heaven destined to raise every believer to unlimited heights. It is a power like no other and is sure to get results.

2 Timothy 1:7: For God hath not given us the spirit of fear; but of power, and of love, and of a sound mind.

As you fellowship with the Holy Spirit, the levels of achievement will be unlimited. Get ready to be filled with:

- The spirit of power
- The spirit of love
- The spirit of a sound mind

You need the spirit of power to cause changes in your life and the lives of others. May power shift you from glory to glory and may nothing stop the move in Jesus Name. Receive this spirit of power as your associate with the Holy Spirit in Jesus Name.

I declare that you will enjoy the spirit of love in Jesus Name. May the spirit of love be poured out on you beyond measure as your build an intimate relationship with the Holy Spirit in Jesus Name.

The spirit of a sound mind will keep you focused and illuminated in a world where darkness seems to be gaining ground. The Spirit of a sound mind causes you to receive and retain God in your mind. It also empowers the realm of godly creativity, I pray His unlimited creativity be opened to you now. May you walk in unusual realms of productivity in Jesus Name. You will see in heavenly colours and achieve uncommon results in Jesus Name.

In this place of fellowship, your spirit will be enthused with eternal powers (Hebrews 6:5) and the more you take time to fellowship with the Holy Spirit in prayer, worship and quiet times of meditation, you will begin to experience a new surge of God's power toward you. Small things will trouble you no more and big things will begin to excite you.

Jesus asked the disciples to wait in the upper room for empowerment and when they did, they shocked their generation (Luke 24:49). My prayer is that as you continue with the Lord, your life will become a testament to the transformational power of God – may you be a shining light for others in Jesus Name.

WHAT DO YOU DO NOW?

Firstly, if you want to give your life to God, you must understand that Christ came to die for all:

2 Corinthians 5:15: He died for everyone so that those who receive his new life will no longer live for themselves. Instead, they will live for Christ, who died and was raised for them.

Why did He die for all? Romans 3:23 gives the answer, 'For everyone has sinned; we all fall short of God's glorious standard.' This state of sin positioned everyone for eternal destruction.

Roman 6:23: For the wages of sin is death, but the free gift of God is eternal life through Christ Jesus our Lord.

God saw this great price and knowing that human kind could not pay, He sent His only son to die and give His life for all.

Roman 10:9-10: If you confess with your mouth that Jesus is Lord and believe in your heart that God raised him from the dead, you will be saved.

For it is by believing in your heart that you are made right with God, and it is by confessing with your mouth that you are saved. The scripture shows if anyone hears of this testimony and believes with all their heart and confesses with their mouth then they have received and will be saved from eternal death and destruction.

Romans 10:13 says that everyone who calls on the name of the Lord will be saved. If you genuinely want to receive Jesus as your Lord and Saviour and become born-again then pray this prayer:

Lord Jesus, I believe with all my heart and I confess with my mouth that you are Lord and Saviour of my life. From today, I confess my sin and repent and receive You – the gift of grace.

Thank you Lord I am now saved. I am born-again and have been made new. I am Your child God and you are my Father!

If you prayed this prayer congratulations! You need to get into the word of God and begin the awesome journey of faith that the Lord has prepared for you! Be at rest and receive the grace, love and faith made available for you to live a victorious life for God in Jesus Name.

Please contact our ministry and share your great news. Remember you are a new creation in Him and more than a conqueror through Him – nothing is impossible with God!

BOOKS BY ALEXANDER O. EMOGHENE

PERFECTING
LOVE
DEFEATING FEAR THROUGH A SIMPLE UNDERSTANDING
OF THE POWER OF GOD'S LOVE
ALEXANDER O. EMOGHENE

Alexander O. Emoghene
HUNGER
FOR
IMPACT
...something is
about to change

Discipleship Curriculum
I WILL BUILD...
Raising The
Next Generation Disciple
A beginners guide to being moulded into
the image of Christ Jesus

ALEXANDER O EMOGHENE
GET IN LINE WITH YOUR
DESTINY
A CALL TO THE JOSHUA GENERATION

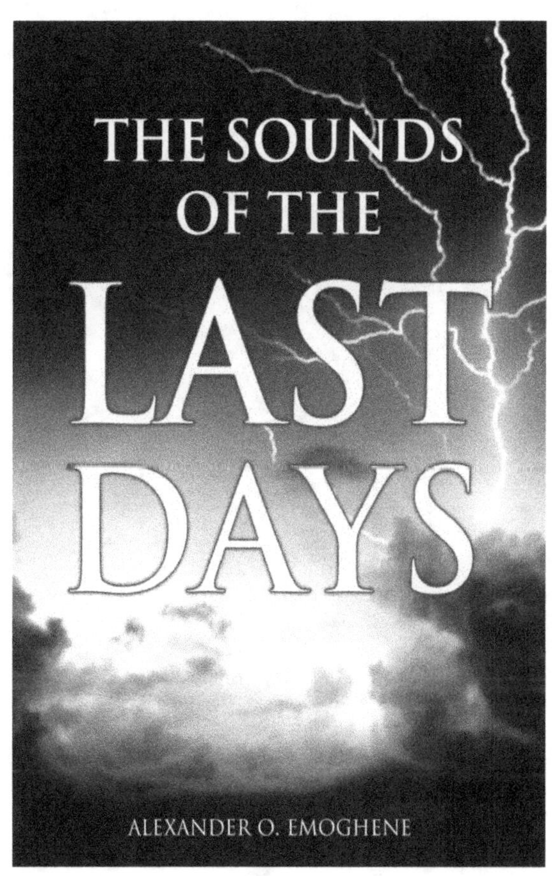

THE SOUNDS
OF THE
LAST
DAYS
ALEXANDER O. EMOGHENE